Eighties

The Fun Years!

Jim Chumley

summersdale

EIGHTIES: THE FUN YEARS!

Summersdale Publishers Ltd
46 West Street
Chichester
West Sussex
PO19 1RP
UK

www.summersdale.com

Printed and bound in China

ISBN: 978-1-84953-117-7

To..

From......................................

You've logged so many miles in
the voyage of life that you've been
upgraded to first class!

Evelyn Loeb

By the time you're eighty years old
you've learned everything. You only
have to remember it.

George Burns

None are so old as those who have
outlived enthusiasm.

Henry David Thoreau

You really haven't changed in seventy
or eighty years. Your body changes,
but you don't change at all.

Doris Lessing

Growing old is a journey best
undertaken with a sense of
humour and curiosity.

Irma Kurtz

After the age of eighty, everything
reminds you of something else.

Lowell Thomas

Being old isn't something to deny, hush up or apologise for. It's something to celebrate.

Virginia Ironside

Growing old is compulsory
– growing up is optional.

Bob Monkhouse

A diplomat is a man who always
remembers a woman's birthday but
never remembers her age.

Robert Frost

Live your life and forget your age.

Norman Vincent Peale

The older I grow the more I distrust
the familiar doctrine that age
brings wisdom.

H. L. Mencken

The best way to get most husbands
to do something is to suggest that…
they're too old to do it.

Anne Bancroft

The oldest trees often bear the
sweetest fruit.

English proverb

Old people shouldn't eat health food.
They need all the preservatives
they can get.

Robert Orben

The follies which a man regrets most in his life are those which he didn't commit when he had the opportunity.

Helen Rowland

Few people know how
to be old.

François de La Rochefoucauld

I think your whole life shows in your face
and you should be proud of that.

Lauren Bacall

If becoming a grandmother was only a matter of choice, I should advise every one of you straight away to become one. There is no fun for old people like it!

Hannah Whitall Smith

It seems that I am living my life backward... at the approach of old age my real youth will begin.

André Gide

To get back my youth I would do
anything in the world, except take
exercise, get up early, or
be respectable.

Oscar Wilde

A man of eighty has outlived probably three new schools of painting, two of architecture and poetry and a hundred in dress.

Lord Byron

Old age is not so bad when you
consider the alternatives.

Maurice Chevalier

What though youth gave love
and roses,
Age still leaves us friends and wine.

Thomas More

Old age ain't no place for sissies.

Bette Davis

There are people who, like houses, are
beautiful in dilapidation.

Logan Pearsall Smith

No man is ever old
enough to know better.

Holbrook Jackson

The three ages of man: youth, middle
age, and 'You're looking wonderful!'

Dore Schary

People ask me what I'd most appreciate getting for my eighty-seventh birthday. I tell them, a paternity suit.

George F. Burns

Anyone who stops learning is old, whether at twenty or eighty. Anyone who keeps learning stays young.

Henry Ford

Text Messaging
for the Elderly

Extra Large Print

One should never trust a woman who
tells her real age. A woman
who would tell one that
would tell one anything.

Oscar Wilde

If I'd known I was going to live this long, I would have taken better care of myself.

Eubie Blake

Men are like wine. Some turn to vinegar, but the best improve with age.

C. E. M. Joad

She's the Iron Lady and I want to be
just like that when I grow up.

Joan Collins on Margaret Thatcher's
eightieth birthday

Children are a great comfort in your old age – and they help you reach it faster, too.

Lionel Kauffman

Sure, I'm for helping the elderly. I'm going to be old myself someday.

Lillian Carter speaking in her eighties

Anyone can get old. All you have to
do is live long enough.

Groucho Marx quoted by the Queen on her
eightieth birthday

It is sad to grow old but nice to ripen.

Brigitte Bardot

I'm not interested in age. People who
tell me their age are silly. You're as old
as you feel.

Elizabeth Arden

I wake up every morning and… look at the obituary page. If my name isn't on it, I get up.

Harry Hershfield

It is not how old you are,
but how you are old.

Marie Dressler

If you can be happy right now, then
you'll always be happy, because it's
always right now.

Willie Nelson

When I was young, I thought that money was the most important thing in life; now that I am old, I know it is.

Oscar Wilde

You are never too old to set another
goal or to dream a new dream.

Les Brown

Red meat and gin.

Julia Child on the key to her longevity

Cosmetics are a boon to every woman, but a girl's best beauty aid is still a near-sighted man.

Yoko Ono

Eighty is when you order a steak and
the head waiter puts it through
the blender.

Bob Hope

Everyone is the age of their heart.

Guatemalan proverb

Old age is the most unexpected of all
the things that can happen to a man.

James Thurber

The more sand has escaped from the hourglass of our life, the clearer we should see through it.

Niccolò Machiavelli

The surprising thing about young fools
is how many survive to become
old fools.

Doug Larson

It takes a long time to
become young.

Pablo Picasso

In many ways, I'm younger than I was
twenty years ago.

Hugh Hefner on turning eighty

I think all this talk about age is foolish. Every time I'm one year older, everyone else is too.

Gloria Swanson

Religion often gets credit for curing
rascals when old age is the
real medicine.

Austin O'Malley

Age is something that doesn't matter,
unless you are a cheese.

Billie Burke

I am… an age when I can only enjoy the last sport left. It is called hunting for your spectacles.

Edward Grey

The longer I live the more beautiful
life becomes.

Frank Lloyd Wright

When grace is joined with wrinkles, it
is adorable. There is an unspeakable
dawn in happy old age.

Victor Hugo

My idea of hell is to be young again.

Marge Piercy

The whiter my hair becomes, the more ready people are to believe what I say.

Bertrand Russell

As a graduate of… Zsa Zsa Gabor School of Creative Mathematics, I honestly do not know how old I am.

Erma Bombeck

The advantage of being eighty years
old is that one has had many
people to love.

Jean Renoir

That's the time of your life when even
your birthday suit needs pressing.

Bob Hope on turning eighty

If the young knew and the old could,
there is nothing that couldn't be done.

English proverb

One of the best parts of growing older? You can flirt all you like since you've become harmless.

Liz Smith

To me, old age is always
fifteen years older
than I am.

Bernard M. Baruch

They say that age is all in your mind.
The trick is keeping it from creeping
down into your body.

Anonymous

How pleasant is the day when we give up striving to be young – or slender.

William James

God, grant me the senility to forget the people I never liked anyway, the good fortune to run into the ones I do, and the eyesight to tell the difference.

Anonymous

When your friends begin to flatter you on how young you look, it's a sure sign you're getting old.

Mark Twain

Oh, to be seventy again.

Georges Clemenceau upon seeing a pretty girl
on his eightieth birthday

It's important to have a twinkle in your wrinkle.

Anonymous

What could be more beautiful than a dear old lady growing wise with age?

Brigitte Bardot

Another belief of mine; that everyone else my age is an adult, whereas I am merely in disguise.

Margaret Atwood

I am a friend of life; at eighty life tells me to behave like a woman and not like an old woman.

Chavela Vargas

The ageing process has you firmly in its grasp if you never get the urge to throw a snowball.

Doug Larson

I've never told anyone how old I am…
So that means I've never once lied
about my age.

Calista Flockhart

There is no old age.
There is, as there always
was, just you.

Carol Matthau

One of the best hearing aids a man can
have is an attentive wife.

Groucho Marx

The older one grows, the more one
likes indecency.

Virginia Woolf

I am long on ideas, but short on time.
I expect to live to be only about
a hundred.

Thomas Alva Edison

Oh, practically everything!

Marie Ponsot on the best thing
about turning eighty

Always be nice to those younger than
you, because they are the ones who will
be writing about you.

Cyril Connolly

Don't let ageing get you down. It's too hard to get back up.

John Wagner

To keep the heart unwrinkled, to be
hopeful, kindly, cheerful, reverent –
that is to triumph over old age.

Thomas Bailey Aldrich

My grandmother is over eighty and still doesn't need glasses. Drinks right out of the bottle.

Henny Youngman

www.summersdale.com